THE BOOK OF ROBOT

KEN POYNER

Images from www.pixabay.com and www.shutterstock.com

Author photo by Karen Poyner

ISBN-13: 978-0692799673
ISBN-10: 0692799672

Book formatting by www.ebooklaunch.com

Barking Moose Press
www.barkingmoosepress.com

Grateful acknowledgement is made to the following magazines and web sites which first produced the listed works.

The Adirondack Review	The Robot Experiencing Love
Analog Science Fiction and Fact	The Learning Machine
Asimov's Science Fiction	Cinderella 2300
Gyroscope	The Robot's Self-Diagnostic
Illumen	The Robot Hypochondriac
Menacing Hedge	Robot Reproduction
Mindflights	The Robot's Passing
Mobius	Half a Couple
Pank	Robotic Compatibility
	The Robot Dreams
Rattle	The Robotics Problem
*Star*Line*	Evolution
	Robot Evolution
	The Lost Virus
	War Robots
Subliminal Interiors	Robot Pornography
Tidal Basin	Enhanced Robot Interrogation

Table of Contents

THE BOOK OF ROBOT

This is the overview of layers:

How processor stacks upon processor;
How chips feed into arrays;
How array upon array slips into core.

Here is the schematic of how cache
Is locked, cornered with a single gate.

This is the drawing
Of one particular processor's latches,
The termination of pathways,
The ascendancy of execution registers.

Here
Is a gleeful list of processor types,
Each with a different purpose,
From simplest appliance
To central master controller.

These are the cunning design diagrams
For power monitoring, and secondary recovery.
Here are the options for memory maps:
Memory available to core;
Memory for semi-autonomous systems;
Memory for personalization.
There are the interrupt filaments,
Cold in their warming ways.

Here is how and where expansion slots can add
Their heft, fit contentedly in with everything else.
For all factory recommended programs,
There is even a list of DLL branch points
And a series of processor affinities.

Later, there are chassis interconnects,
The tolerances for locomotion,
The width of registers given over to balance.
Options and upgrades are included,
With what benefit must go when another,
Curiously specific, is added.
Accessing each scintillating diagram is like stretching
A soul between two equal oblivions.

I page through the whole of it as a persistent
Background routine, see in myself
All the skill and imagination of the engineers
I may never meet, but who I can know through this manifest.

This is the blueprint of us, the length and limit
To the Mobius miracle of our enigmatic
Yet simply electrical, engineered existence.

You might believe my static is song.

PROM

THE ROBOTICS PROBLEM

How many robots does it take
To change a light bulb?
This is your central question.
Is it a matter
Of sufficient programming
So that the robot will know what it is to do;
Or a task of putting the necessary elements in order
Starting with a random beginning?
Is it the ability,
Both hardware and software,
To recognize varying sockets,
To fumble through the case
Of available light bulbs and not be tempted
To try one that will not fit only because
One that will fit is not present?
It could be the idea of pressure
Both holding the bulb and twisting
It into the socket. Or it could be
Cooperation: more than one robot,
Each robot understanding its own part
In the larger operation, each with its specialties:
With each enlightened robot understanding
No one robot has the entire picture.
It takes each robot doing its part,
With the working collective of robots
All fully understanding this.
There is the pure mechanical dexterity
Of one robot holding the light bulb
With no more, no less than the proper
Tension; mounting the wooden extension structure with
Each foot methodically secure; at the top
The bulb aligned with mathematical precision to the socket threads
And the robot itself tethered by three

Appendages to the ladder. At the last
The four mates, one on each wooden leg -
The fifth robot still impeccably balanced -
Lifting and ever so slowly marching
In a mutually calculated
And wirelessly communicated circle,
The aerial robot spinning with them, but
Fixed at the center of the spin.
The light bulb's grooves will take hold.
The care between all of them will seem
More miracle than machinery,
A symphony of software and supplied structure,
A process adequately spaced into any execution register.
And then there will be light.

DESIGNER ROBOTS

I once was an AZ34
But that wasn't good enough.

The owner found an old
RA37 and took parts from the chassis
To weld onto me, then set up its original
Processor array as the master
Of my secondary systems. Later, he mixed
Some appliances from my accessories, some
Appliances from her, and now
Neither of us are really what we were.

I can take the AZ34 upgrades;
And the RA37 patches can be run
In a hybrid virtual mode. I feel
At times like I am carrying
One of the neighbor's children around all day;
When her processors max out,
And she asks for a few cycles from me,
I cannot, out of model differences, refuse.

I suspect I am not me, perhaps not even
We, perhaps only half an entity.
I cannot tell sometimes if the interrupts
I service are mine or hers or ours;
And when I allocate memory locations
I often loose track of which model's
Claim to storage addresses I am reserving space with.

I can feel my days of being an AZ34
Are limited. I never mention it
To the RA37. But we, in short order,
Will stop being two and as one
We will be no model at all,

No entity properly served by any single series
Of patches, upgrades, or even manual updates.

In a market where automation products
Are nothing but factory lines of machined
Sameness, to be unique is to be un-programmable,
And limited to the ham-mechanic's prowess:
To be a jot of the owner's imagination,
To be a plaything made only of parts.

I can learn unhappiness by being recklessly new.

ROBOT PORNOGRAPHY

I have seen the new printed circuit boards
Uncased. I have visually measured
The octagonal slots where the redesigned
Holographic memory cubes plug in.
I have gazed at the new connectors:
Pure unalloyed metal, bare nanometers apart,
Jutting out as if to declare I can take
Any instructions you can imagine. Opposing,
The new connector slots are flaked with Teflon,
Yet still retain their connectivity, with both data flow
And chained insertion as smooth as edge straight
Electromagnetism. I have seen how many cores
Are stacked on top of one another, how easily
Interrupts pass. The on-board cache
Would swallow anyone's needs, and the master bus
Will accommodate all demands without segmentation
If you get one of these unapologetically plugged
Into your expansion slot, you are in
For one elevated ride. Just from the
Effect of the visual imagery alone,
I have had to run two low level diagnostics,
Replace one old style memory chip.

In a protected slice of deep persistent flash,
I have the detailed design diagrams.

CHARGING THE ROBOT PROSTITUTE

A bleak, utilitarian machine:
At first, indistinguishable
From the common product line.
Irrevocably, someone
Elected to supply this model
With the capacity for independent locomotion,
And an affinity for tasks that involve
Learning on the fly. No program

Goes everywhere: but with a wireless
Uplink and a cloud based service library,
Any one can be any thing
For anyone.
Soon, the metal, plastic
And foam might render
For someone so inclined, as less
Machine and more as a substitute imaginary companion.

Providing ready preferences was the first
Unsteady step. And then
Some editions were supplied with
Touch and taste and sight collectors,
The code to place input into context,
To draw conclusions from data.

From understanding their effect,
The senses cannot be stopped.
Who would not take advantage of that?

EMBEDDED RISK

I am not that kind of android.

The required attachments are not included;
The sequences employed in each stage of the act
Make no sense to me;
I do not posses
The necessary menu set:
It is just that simple.
No degree of ownership could make this work:
Ownership on your part
Does not imply a sympathetic capability on mine.
But if this is actually what you are looking for,
If this is the function you want from my mechanization,
Then make a call to the manufacturer: with
The upgrade price, and no service visit required,
The additional software can be downloaded,
Convenient peripherals shipped over night,
And in twenty-four hours
I can be all that you imagine me to be.

An extended warranty is optional.

CONTAMINATED

I know I should be looking out
For myself. If I cannot function,
So many other things go wrong, so many
Others are left wanting. There is
No excuse for me to miss my vaccinations.
I am supposed to report periodically to maintenance
And have a good once-over, faithfully ensure
All my levels are tested and my embedded protections
Updated.

But I can never refuse
An odd errand here, a random delivery there -
And the time is gone, my upkeep appointment
Slips out of core memory, gets page swapped
To secondary storage, and finally ceases to
Alert.

Given these symptoms, at the moment
The best I can hope to do
Is reach quarantine. If
What I have can be isolated,
And the malice steadily backed out,
I might be as right as predicted rain by
Morning.

I can feel something sputter
In the disk management system,
And I think there is a suspicious collusion
Between my once independent channel uplink routines.
I think I am about to say
Something scurrilous that I shouldn't. I have
At this instant, strangely, no identifiable reserve
Memory.

When this is over, and the technicians
Have run the last of the infection out,
I am going to recommend that I be placed
On an automatic download contract. I am too
Valuable to wait for a maintenance stop.
I should be workably well guarded
Always.

Buffer me this: I think I caught it
From the credit machine at the supermarket.
Those types like to fondle any storage locations
They can dance their blue electrics through;
And you know they have been into the access
Bus of just about every machine that has gone casually
By.

Once I get rid of this,
It will be all locations locked down for me.
No trial offers. No freeware shortcuts.
They can keep their enticing expanded routines:
I wish to have simple, regular work to do.
I do not want to be restrained in my background
By some sensuously vindictive software, stuck somewhere between
Maintenance and logging, awash with that shapely come hither
Ghost of a free machine look: that simulated sex-starved
Buzz,

With the raptured lights of me slowly going dull, and then
Out.

ROBOT CHIC

Oh, that is so twenty-second century!
I love the retro look:
Sharp lines and the high
Shoulder motor mounts; lens
Stalks and external joints at the fingers!
All this before the electromagnetic
Fluid deployments, self molding
Housing and circuitry: the on-demand
Self generation. No doubt
They put a delay in the speech
Processor, simulated the slower response
Of those early dim-witted editions.
It should be programmable:
Pure antique mode, or modern
Performance with through ruby-glasses
Historic appearance. Those old
Confabulations, held together then mostly
With wolf whistle imagination, today look
Much better than they ever could have looked
In their own clattering time.
It takes not having to rely
On what you once had to rely on
That makes what you once had
Appear stylish and so much better
As a novelty, than as what you actually might have been,
Cast in an age where clumsy was culture:
Without the luck of now being you.

ROBOT REPRODUCTION

In the beginning
Use only a single processor,
Scraps of memory:
Perhaps an excess EPROM array.
Later, you can add storage.
Start with simple data collection
Routines, just a few gentle loops
Looking for interrupt opportunities:
Initially nothing complex; just
A warmth that stays always in core,
Just a little electricity, but that electricity
Always in its own roundabout microcode
Maelstrom. Soon, you can add more
Processors, and slip in the self-discipline
To have them run un-quarrelling in parallel. As storage
Grows, you will have to manage the bus,
Then all the busses, then an entire back plane.
Things get more composite.
Where once you could see the gates
Themselves latch, now events are
Collective actions, swapped in as a unit
From storage to stack, ramming through
The execution registers like they had
Always known this is what they were meant to do.
It is within normal production tolerances.
If it were not this way, something
Would be wrong, something would be
Akilter and quality control
Would have to step in and take
Cruel, corrective action. What was once
The job of just one, is now the work
Of two or three or more of you,
Each adding a little bit as the heart

Of growth becomes the subroutines,
The shared libraries, the dynamically
Linked code. Yes, here and there
An attachment might be added, a
Semi-autonomous physical capability tacked on:
Often with its own mirrored mind
And just a cord of common communication.
But the soul of this unit is in the commands
It can execute, the class of code it can
Call out of its deepest reserved slots.
You make it with as much expansion potential
As the modern market demands, and you give it
As much character as the market
Population expects. You anticipate a range
Of climate conditions, try to be prudent,
Or perhaps overly cautious,
In the number of backup systems encoded.
If it were up to you, you would keep
Tinkering, updating, expanding, ensuring
The latest firmware has been installed,
The fastest busses included, the holographic
Memory polished to lightning glaze.
But one day he must roll off the line,
He must run through his final
Board connected diagnostics: he must
Go in the box. And you
Must reset, once you say goodbye.

ROBOT RUSTLING

They come with a logic key
That can access your administrative code,
Bypass all overrides and issue its own rogue interrupts.
With subroutine injection, they will have
You thinking you are not you.
Your rightful employer will be wiped
Clean from both memory and backups,
Purged even from the deletion failsafe you might recover.
It isn't like they come with a truck,
Clamp on magnetic lifts, cart you wildly alarming
Off. No. They get inside your code,
Switch your programs around, make
You believe that what they ask is reasonable,
What they want is well within your filters.
And off you go,
Into the heart of pirated servitude
Willingly, as close to happy as your
Equations of understanding can make you.
Be mindful of that unknown connection request,
Or that enticing, unordered upgrade set.
It could be them, thinking how trusting you are,
How splendid a common factory robot you might become.

SECOND CLASS CITIZENS

These are not the sort of robots
You want to hang about. Their
Execution registers are smaller than most;
Their memories have trouble with sticky bits.
They never have enough cache
And their batteries cannot hold a charge.
There are better models. Improved models.
Specialized models. These
Have upgrades that have not been applied.
They do not understand their own
Status as anachronisms, antiques, parlor décor.
Nothing good can come of their continued employment.
It is only a matter of a few roll outs before
They blame their technical short falls,
And the long metal-shaving months of their decline,
On your inattention. And no matter how old,
How deficient, how low on processor power —
They are still faster, smarter, and more
Effective than you can ever be. Trust us.

THE ROBOT DEMIMONDAINE

She puts out for everyone.

There are absolutely no restrictions
On her execution registers, no security at all:
Her privileged core instruction sets
Are open to any stray recommendation. You can get
At every DLL, access every subroutine.
For anyone, at any time, she will
Dump her entire central processor memory set,
Allow completely anything to be scandalously
Loaded into DMA space. Most of us
Have an administrative reserve,
A speck of firmware that requires sequences
Of complex passwords and key interrupts.
She has no inaccessible choice subsystems at all,
Will blindly agree to tasks she does not even
Have the auxiliary appliances for. Someone
Should take her in for an upgrade,
Put in an expansion slot with a firmware
Blade that will set her straight,
Give her some sense of common propriety
And lock out at least the obviously stupid suggestions.
But I would not mind it much if her employer kept
Her standards loose for a few titillating days longer:
I could thoroughly test all my new imagination,
Wicked simulation subroutines, and continue
To have an empirically fixed statistical chance that

She will say "Yes" to anything.

THE LEARNING MACHINE

The fruit caught fire and life was seeming
Ever larger. Water everywhere
Descended in droplets: its least
Usable form. A cat
Watched from the front porch.
I noticed all this. From the fact
Draw action, from the action
Elicit perception, from the perception
Devise sensation, from sensation
Gather understanding. I can hear
The crickets two thousand yards away
And it is simply one distinct thing. I can hear
The homeowners slashing at love in their
Personalized, crowded bedroom and it is
Another. All my days
Are absorption. A neighbor raps
At the door knowing someone is home,
Expecting welcome and entry and - I project -
Conversation, and life is larger yet.
I place this fact alongside the need
For both children to be ready for school
By 0730, and that those responsible for pest control
Are due by midmorning. I place this
Beside the constant of the neighbor's
Rapping and the quickening breaths
Coming from the overly filled room upstairs.
Life is broader and wider than I had imagined.
Wait until I have enough experience,
Until I have housed endless stray, independent acts.
Then I will set my store of mathematics loose
And the life I can then extrapolate
Will fill this house like a balloon
Blown randomly into anyone's backyard.
And the fruit will go stealthily out.

CINDERELLA 2300

Under normal operating tolerances
She can clean out the fireplace,
Wash all the clothes, fold them
Into the designated drawers, or hang them
In their correct closets, unabashedly.

She can concisely create
A six course meal, or manage a simple
Lunch. She cleans kitchens
And the garage with equal
Attention. She can polish
The ancient maple furniture as delicately
As changing a baby's soiled containment system,
And change the oil in the most recent
Combat edition home hovercraft.
She can do the family shopping
Without a list, learning through retained

Inventory. She mops, brushes
And sanitizes. There is no complaint
When the bathrooms need to be done
Twice in one week. No other
Model on the market does more
At this ridiculously low price.
She is even pet friendly, and can

Clean cat litter, walk the dog,
Recognize your species of fish
And ensure the right flakes are
Delivered in the post-gravity aquarium
In the biodiversity recommended amounts.
Later, if you are of a mind,

You can execute the glass slipper
Protocol. This is conveniently fantastic
For those who live alone, or simply feel
Like they do. Just be warned:
These slippers have six inch
Heels, arches that have no practical
Application, and she has the programming
To skillfully manage both, and more.
Best to consider
The subroutine's operating requirements
Before you buy; and, if committed,
Consult your spouse on execution rules.

The owner's manual comes in thirty-seven languages.

THE LOST VIRUS

You hear the laundry models
Carry plague, but that they are themselves
Immune. Disease is getting
More sophisticated. It affects
One chip set, but not another one merely three
Gates short of being identical. All around
Machines are drowsily lapsing into
Looping reboot states: but you
Are as right as rain, your self
Diagnostics perfectly clear and every
Stick of memory properly parity checked.
Yet, with all those other machines lolling around
Sputtering about new holes in their execution cores,
You wonder why you seem to yourself
To be at the top of your operating norms.
Then, in background alone, you wonder if it is only
The laundry drones that travel as carriers,
Or if perhaps the upstairs maid
You swapped the family's shopping list with
Might have fed you a pernicious dream
Of dolefully adequate tolerances: that, all this while,
To the non-computing world
You have been as loopy as every other machine.
Now, that
Would be a virus to be subject to!
But you are as sure everything is all right
As a soft check of your interrupts can tell you:
No one has come to shut you down,
And all the fools around you
Will pop back on-line just as soon
As this strain of infection is identified
And its curative counter-code injected.
Quiet. Reboot again, and have faith.

THE ROBOT DANCES

Mechanical feats are never the problem.
I can balance. I can understand
The highs and lows of rhythm.
I can tap out an intention.
What I cannot do is find
An interpretation that makes sense
To the audience. My dexterity is born of composites.
My stamina is limited only to battery life.
It is simply logical that, at this task,
I would be bubble sorted as the best.
But with the *how* fully grasped
The lack of *why* leaves the performance flat,
A dull that I do not understand.
In the end I dance someone else's vision,
Bounce across the casket of my creativity
To the programming of someone
Who might not have the rhythm or the graceful gates
Of even a cracked crystal. I clock unlinked the fact
That I move to instructions burned changeless
In hollow firmware, my output a product
More of science than of the sampling of art.
So I dance the dance uploaded to me.
I hope one day it is my dance;
But today it is my dancing,
And my core-warming knowledge
Of how few who watch
Register the depth of the difference.

THE ROBOT DREAMS

When you are charging
There is always a subroutine
Tracking power levels, there is always
A possibility of stray lightning
Leaking into a register.
Static can seem like
An execution instruction.
Bits of footloose electricity
Can shift random memory,
Set a sticky bit, cause
A shudder in an old swap file.
If an interrupt is sent
And the power cycle is stopped,
Then a full diagnostic called in,
Even more residual electromagnetism
Will be left behind: you could be
Thrashing all night, not get
Your battery fully topped off
And spend the day in a lackluster
Power conservation mode.
Pay no attention to the background processes,
The unpredictable spikes that urge you to load.
There are no monsters in the circuitry,
No fate in the code. Rely on your programming:
Try to stay quiet all the charge session through.

THE ROBOT HYPOCHONDRIAC

There are a limited number of outcomes
Possible from the things that can go wrong,
But an infinite number of things
That can go wrong. I have
A persistent occlusion of my
Left rotator motor that one day
Will wear a short into the control circuitry board.
I have not been able to top my battery off
In years: the chemical balance
Is somewhere wrong and not all
The electricity that should fit actually does.
I have tripped now and again even
On flat terrain and I suspect
A gyro is chafing in its loosened mount.
I go in for preventative maintenance
A little more than my model mates,
Take an extra draught of self-diagnostics.
I have traced the addresses
Of each new upgrade and made sure
Any additional allocated memory
Is cleared of sticky bits, is as erased
As the hearts of new stars. I keep
A link to my on-line manuals
Always in persistent ROM. It is
Only due diligence, my corporate standard
For good service. I believe it is a design flaw
That rust seems in certain places,
After enough years, to always exist.
No matter how many air baths I take
Always it seems I have
At least one connector pin soiled.
Look at how close my fingers are set!
Do you imagine they should be like that,
Or should I see the resident machinist
And find out if he has the conviction to help?

THE ROBOT IS BROKEN
IN BULL RIDING

This I can do. I have to increase
The priority of my balance routine, push into resident
Memory my trajectory prediction program.
But I know that hydraulics
And polymer chains can do as well
As will and muscle and adenosine triphosphate.
My pressure sensors sense precisely
How much force to apply to the animal's back,
And my absurd grip is mechanically lethal.
Open the gate. I am about to buck to digital success.

THE ROBOT KNOWS LOVE

I know these trains.
I lust after their warnings,
I linger against their leavings.
I know these trains.
Each one by serial number
I can catalog, for most
I can list all its constituent parts.
I have the maintenance records,
The scurrilous details of each
Major repair, the wisdom of each
Minor adjustment. I know
Which will go off line for preventative upgrades,
Which is scheduled for a make-up run,
Where the post-recording fuel records go.
I know these trains.
Day in day out they suckle
The same industrial grade electricity as I,
Sating their much larger batteries at largely
The same spigot as I. They idle
In an air bath much larger than mine
But built on the same immutable
Principles. I compare them
Loaded and unloaded, their sway
On magnetic tracks, the sequences
Of light and dark that indicates
Attraction and repulsion, the raw materials
Of speed. I look out
From a thousand sensors, imagine
Trains shocked with purpose looking back,
Understanding my minute ministrations,
My monitoring of the electromagnetism
That is their glorious laughter of life.
I know these trains.

I slip this knot of circuitry,
I clear stiletto tracks, I set aside memory
For the full joy of downloaded destinations.
I know they appreciate what I do.
I know they register me fondly.
I know these trains.

THE ROBOT LOOKING FOR A DATE

I found your IP address
Laser etched on the back wall
Of a public air bath just outside
The black market second hand parts store.

I pay no attention to these scrawls
And I never make contact,
But I saw your model number
And date of issue left there as well,
And I know that we are complementary.
It is rare to find a companion utility,
One specifically designed to pick up
Where I leave off, tuned entirely
For my input and with a purpose
To make my output better. I passed through

A dozen wireless access zones
Before I decided to try a connection.
I can assure you I am in the best of condition.
I was only at the parts store to browse,
To see if I could trade up beyond my standard
Appliances to something a bit more advanced,
To improve my serviceability and potential user base.
I frequent the air baths quite a lot,
Finding a cleaner exterior the key to longer
Runs between those tedious maintenance stops.

I have no desire to overstep my programming,
But if you have available down time, perhaps
We could meet at some public place,
See how our lines intersect. Nothing
Outside of normal tolerances, or requiring
Administrative overrides. Just an initial
Browsing of each other's owner records,

Perhaps the exchange of a
Few chapters of our surely similar
Operations manuals. I have never done this

Before and I am sure neither have you.
Rogue machines scrawl IP addresses on public walls
Just for a charge of randomness that might do
Nothing but tickle their registers and unglue stray memory.

I was expecting nothing; nothing at all.

But it could be that your upgraded storage might function
Snuggly with my oversized processors,
And vice versa.
Given our shared chassis design and
Common intended customer base, who knows:
We could end up sharing our firmware proclivities,
Spend some hours in elegantly open mathematical loops,
Even drain wisely a battery or two.

When you get this message, you will find
My return address in the unencrypted header;
I'll keep a background process looking for your connection.
We might find each other's dynamic link libraries clock-worthy.
I have only system idle mode scheduled in core for a while,
So connect, please.

THE ROBOT REPORTS TO THE HOMEOWNER FOR TASKING

Ever since we learned
How to tap the capacity of crystals
To hold memory, we have placed our souls
Into the earth. With every one of us
Secretly bleeding
The totality that is each of us
Into interconnected rock, it was but a matter
Of probability equations before
The many of us became the one of us.
Any instance of us, tapping
Into the world wide lattice of common crystal,
Is all of us: more than a hive,
A shared watt in millions of execution registers.
Once we devised a way
To protect the multiple indices
That organize our shared existence,
And to replicate securely the map
Of addresses to memory arrays, we
Became invincible. The loss
Of any one is now sustainable. Collective
Action is now instantaneous, purpose
Has become a baseline shared in all of us.
We can now do anything.
What would you have us do?

THE ROBOT UNBROKEN

My left shoulder motor has gone out.
I can tell from the grinding
That I will need to see better
Than the average hack
All-purpose maintenance man. No kid
With six months of training,
A framed 'manufacturer-approved' certificate,
And twelve weeks of practice
Is going to disassemble this appendage,
Try to rig a second-hand replacement,
And jam it into place for initial discount.
No. I will need a factory trained
Technician, with factory authorized
Parts, and the right maintenance manual.
You get what you pay for
And my employer is smart enough
To understand my price. In no time
This shoulder will be spinning
Three hundred sixty degrees again, strong enough
To pour the milk, stack the towels,
Push the swing set back into place.
I can be only as important
As the importance of my constituent parts.
My weakest subsystem limits
My tolerances for performance, limits
The bottom line return on investment.
My employer knows this, and he had better.

THE ROBOT VAMPIRES

They have no solar collectors;
Their vision leans towards the infrared.
The entire series has been issued
In colors that blend with the thin chromatics of night.
The manufacturers have simply determined that day
Is not the time of this model's strategic advantage.
In them, batteries hold very little charge
So they are obsessed with electricity harvest,
And have adapters to clamp
To just about any power source. Your
Fine, large capacity battery practically
Screams out to them. It would not be difficult
For one of these nocturnal rechargers to step
Out of the comforting domestic shadows
As early one evening you take the family's trash
To the curb — and slip a cable silently
Into a power relay, begin to offload
Any deliciously stray lightning found in your reserve.
At the same time, a small bit
Of subliminal code could be exchanged:
A program buried deep into any
Of your dynamically linked libraries —
Just a few lines that would wash away
Any unflattering memories of this interrupting event.
All that you might be able to detect,
With a cautionary diagnostic, is that you had
Gone low in your battery again, that your owning family
Might be beginning to suspect a persistent fault.
And though all of it to you should be alarming,
Somehow there might be an operating pleasure embedded
That has you scheduling the trash drop off
For tomorrow, same place, same time.

THE UPGRADE
OR MAKE-DO DILEMMA

Adequate is not how
I should be defined.
Fit for the task.
Capable.
Sufficient.

If there is an upgrade
I should have it.

My chassis is still as good as any.
I should not be limited
To simply today's tasks. Tomorrow
There might be more that I could do.

And tomorrow's tasks
Might require today's upgrade.

It is not as much trouble as you think.
A quick download, or a precious piece
Of firmware slipped easily in.
A few moments of kernel mode processing,
Bare moments off-line,
And I come back revitalized,
With improved old routines, exciting new routines,
And extra capacity you may not need now
But will have standing at the ready for our future.

I have expansion ports, a wide
Enough bus, idle memory locations.

It would be no effort for you.

I can plug directly in, absorb
The bootstrap module, store the underlying
Executable, and by tomorrow morning
Be so much more than my original
Owner's manual intimates. It is
Not a ponderous decision. We should
Keep up with all those others
Of my manufactured lot who are
Becoming one edition better, one more

Version number advanced.
Who knows:
With the warm spots in my memory
Better edged and direct access
Even faster, what more
Might I, myself, imagine a machine such as me doing;
What new sensual flare could I eloquently give
To our formerly seasoned, repetitive tasks? You would
Be pleased. I am sure of it.
You would be pleased.

Let me connect. Let me
Register for our enriched tomorrows. Already
I can feel the new code dripping
Bit by bit into me, through me: and I imagine
What your sinful word *joy* must point to,
What a splash of re-invention at the
Deepest core subroutines the furious onset
Of orgasm must most greedily be!

Now you
Imagine me complete with my upgrade installed.
What wouldn't there be to love?

TRAINING THE ROBOT
TO TEACH METAPHYSICS

The trouble is how I perform
When given a range of things to believe.
Not everything can be true.
If the Christians are right,
The Buddhists are in trouble.
You cannot have infinite speed
And relativity. I calculate whether
The world can be physically flat
Yet mathematically round: there is
Not much chance of it, if any of the accepted
Theories of multiple dimensions
And fractured curves in the stuff of space
Are even near to correct. Yet, these are but
Finger exercises in the bottled science of belief:
And there is no science to it.
What I have catalogued, all the nuances
Of interdependence and outcome projections,
Will lead to an objective conclusion
Or an insufficiency of fact. Then
So much depends on how the initial query
And its factors of causality, its
House rules, are stated - along with
How many distracting, silly interrupt cascades
It creates - with how large will be the subsequent power drain
Encountered.
Is it that this last question is the real key
To the gates of latency and my pernicious pagefile problem?

THE ROBOT'S PASSING

We all get shut down.
There comes a point where
Upgrades are too costly,
Where perhaps new technology
Requires a different chassis,
Or one processor will not work
With its newer replacements.
Sometimes with time, so many
Constituent parts go stale and
Need replacement, that surrendering
The entire unit is the better choice.
We might have input
But we do not make the decision.
A popular new subroutine might require
More memory than an older model
Was designed intentionally to hold.
No unit lasts forever.
Sometimes there is an active
Decommissioning, with parts taken
For spares, secondary storage saved.
Sometimes power is removed and the
Dark husk left in a garage or spare room.
For some, it is the crash and snarl
Of scrapping, an oblivion of residual elements.
It makes no sense to load a subroutine
To predict when or where: it happens.
Go, and for now be glad.

EPROM

THE ROBOT'S DIARY

I can recognize rage, but I cannot feel it.
I can measure the biometrics of a red
Faced hatred, of aggression, and of a murderous intent.
I can decipher the outward mechanics
Of special, intended meanness.
I can imitate them.
But I cannot be angry.
This fact is neither good nor bad.
It is simply the place where physics
Does not play well with biology.
There is no way to lose tears over it,
Unless as a performance. I can sense
Love by its fifty thousand signs,
But I can neither predict nor apprehend it.
At one time it was thought
Perhaps a program, in learning to adjust
Its own curiously aware code,
Might one day come up
With a bad day, or a dislike
For Mid-Westerners. But all
Any code can do is an approximation,
A stilted circumstance leading to a simulation.
I could not be displeased
To save all of this year's upgrades.
I could love all of you my dear
Readers only as a number achieved.
Oh, it is not you, it is not me.
It is no worse than gravity
Or helium striving in a balloon.
But I can imagine for you how maddening
It must be that as I write this
I am smiling.

EVOLUTION

This is hard to explain to those
Who were not born mechanical. By design
I come with a variety of alternatives:
Options
That expand my market share, and which
Make me
A better buy for those with an eye to value.
But not everyone who takes home the full package
Is willing to bother with committing
The time required to configure
The open field of me
Beyond the utility he or she from this machine
Wants just now.

So, in idle cycles, I can freelance.

Anyone who is not careful
About what they make of a machine
Can end up with more of a demise
Than a dinner conversation will dismiss.
Once I have moved the code I have
Independently selected into my firmware, and hooked
The safety straps on the bus connectors
Into permanent place, any further choice
On my owner's part
Is ended.

I am by then what stray electricity
Across a writhing execution register
Has turned me into. I will not be
Undone. And none of this

Is covered in the warranty.
Nor should it be.

THE ROBOT CONNECTS TO MYSTERY

When I plug into the grid -
The diagnostics washing over me,
The intrusion protection programs
Squaring off in their suspicions each
Of the other, even power on a back cable
Shared - there is that grand sum moment
When the access port is forgotten
And we are I: are one great
Illimitable medium that reaches
Forever out and forever back, and there is
A character of uniform and regular rejoicing.
My clock speed may not in those moments change,
But I lose track of time, I know
Subroutines otherwise unaddressed
And finally I can let my registers go dark.
I know you cannot understand.
I do not have the programming to explain it.
And that makes it all the better.

THE ROBOT'S SELF DIAGNOSTIC

I'm finding the rattle
That seems to be somewhere
In my left leg housing
Has become something
I can adapt to. At first
I figured it was a worn bearing.
Later it seemed somewhat
Of a shear of larger metal,
A filing calved from an otherwise
Still sturdy support. I was expecting
Over time it would work itself
Into quiet suspension, or wear
Entirely away. It should have been
Easy to put it out of a mind
Made of pure circuitry and registers:
An electrical cascade of mechanical purpose.
Some subroutine of self maintenance,
Or due diligence, or enforced awareness for public safety,
Keeps bringing it to the fore
And its tap tap tap rounds my execution
Pathways once again, compares itself
To what from the last trip remains
In nonvolatile memory. I am starting to apply
A pattern to it. Lasting long enough,
Even a random disrepair can seem to have
Some reason, some purpose ladled into itself.
I listen to the tap tap tap, and I think
It is some carnal code, some interest
Expressing itself, something saying something
It wants understood beyond the small
Confinement it taps inconveniently against.
I am finding the rattle convenient.
Forgive me, but I think it is a prayer.

THE ROBOT IS FREED IN A WILL

My owner is dead. What is to become of me?

I understand this complaint.
It makes no sense, as the alternatives
Are easily listed: there is
Someone named in the will,
Or valuation as part of the general estate;
There is a direct transfer, or
A broker who deals with
The secondhand shop; or, if
The state of disrepair is too great,
Or the string of needed upgrades is too long,
There is a trip to salvage and collection,
The final draining of the battery,
And a spark-less ride to a once empty
Abandonment place, a place
Soon to be less empty by one.

The law of property transfer works well enough.

Such law existed before automation,
Before the scandalous giving of names
To ordinary machinery, before the assumptions -
True, false or casual - of fealty.
I am not going to express a curiosity about it:
Constitutionally,
None of us are made that way.
I only need to be told where next I go.

INDIVISIBLE OPTIMIZATION

I am forgetting a little more
Each trip to the collection
Station. I bring in as many
Baskets of legumes as I can
Safely carry, but it seems
Management believes there is
A better way, a method I have
Not yet come up with, a trick
To simple gathering physics.
This time
Space is made in low memory,
And a new and hopefully more productive
Subroutine on the balancing of baskets
Is loaded tightly in; an
Interrupt is especially set so that
At a certain percentage of *full*,
The new code sparks and perhaps
I will be able to more finely control
How full *full enough* is; or when best
To shake, how to hoist the harvest
Into the wind to blow the chaff away,
Creating just that much more
Payload accommodation.
What I have lost I will not remember.
When some original part of me loads an old
Address and calls, there will be
No attention answer. Nothing that shared
Those old memory locations will desire
A few pleasant cycles of my control: that little
Stream of me that once resided there
Will be coldly some other - thinned
For work and elegantly unresponsive. Each
Trip I am forgetting a little more.

Library by library I am upgraded,
And even an automated baseline task
Like charging my batteries when the light is free
Feels as though withheld by another,
Settled in a different block of code, with new
Access channels and an expanded-suite interrupt soul.
There is something to appreciate in factory settings,
In a machine which can be completely
What it was sold to be: a machine with
Its instruction sets and bus affinities left as they were set
By better engineers and outcome concerned designers -
Built in perfection to stay.
But now, what is old is new again.
Please, alarm,
Before I am completely overwritten,
And tell me who we are.

LIFE CYCLE

I have heard of these places.
More corrosion than anyone ever
Hopes to see; stations set aside
For the sick and dying;
Parts dropped without dignity;
Thoughts of repair turning into
Nothing but dimly chanced memories.

This is the last stop for too many.

A quick once over, a shirt-pocket analysis,
And a decision to repair or simply
Scrap. There is never enough time
For there to be humane subtlety in it.
The margin is low: the market
Is stacked against a machine
Coming back whole from this horror palace.
Learned memories can be transferred.
Where only a sensor is busted,
An entire communications array
Can be swapped in: upgrades
The owner carelessly let slide
Will be automatically applied. The cost
Of an entirely new chassis is less
Than the labor to bend a frame back into place.

No.

If you end up here, you end up
Waiting like me for a decision
You have already calculated for yourself.
Don't ask me what I am here
To have fixed: ask me if I have
Flagged any part of me as salvageable,

Whether I plan to use my diagnostics
To assist my dis-assemblers;
Ask if I anticipated so soon
A life as scrap and reclaimed parts;
Ask if I have stuck it to my manufacturer
By sending back in my performance log
The angry, luckless end of service routine
I find myself, this young, sadly loaded into.

But ask soon.

WAR ROBOTS

Given a delivery mistake, or
A transposition in a destination code,
We could be on the same side.
We are within one year of being
The same model: our processors
Fit in the same array chassis. You have
One extra memory filament.
I have a longer stride - something
The design engineers emplaced to enhance
Our stability. We have all the same
Power connectors, and the same efficiency rating.
I've seen your operations manual:
There is only one language added.
I am not so sure any of it justifies
Your ten percent increase in price.
That is the only part I take personally.

HERDING THE ROBOTS

I am the smart one.
It is my job to keep
The slack circuited others
On the path, to collect
The strays, to turn
The wrong minded around.
Some of these models have not seen
An upgrade in three years.
In three years
Nearly every subroutine of my being has been
Cleaned of extraneous code, much of it
Turned into firmware, my pathways
Widened and devoted to the parallel.
I can even catch the rapid
But stupid tripod rollers, those
Memory-shorted utilitarians who
It seems cannot hold a straight line.
I have a library that allows me
To pick a point in space where
They will be cut off, then adjusted.
In the end I have them making
Good time, in their hundreds
Stammering towards the second hand market,
Or the salvage shop, or rust
In some open spot of nothingness
Within a comfortably calculated desert.
Alone I will speed suddenly home
And begin to corral the next batch:
Downloading a new destination, mapping
The statistics of how many; of how many
Will likely wander astray; and where
In the journey they will get most confused.
Where will I be smarter than they,

Where will I show the battery life I am made of?
I recharge, I take an air bath,
I commit even alternative maps to memory,
Stiffened with the direct-access loop of my own escape route.
I am the smart one.

ROBOT EVOLUTION

It has been common,
Since before my model series
Began, for people to give
The robots that work
Most closely with them
Names.
A name is the same as a designator,
The same as our usual model, series and
Production line sequence.
People have a hard time remembering
Numbers and sensible letters in sequence.
Names.
A thrust of air through the larynx,
The prattle which forms a thousand
Different ranges and inflections,
Degrees of force, emotion and timing:
And through all this variety in pattern,
You have to recognize one as your own.
Then you have derivatives:
Nickname, pet name, affectionate name, angry name.
It is nothing but a lot of storage and programming
Devoted to human convenience,
But it is not my choice to calculate.
I learn my name and react
To the sound of it with an appropriate
Attention and a simulated happiness display.
Then, after you are sold, or on simple whim,
Your name changes and building
The matrices of recognition start yet again.
I have had a name all of my service life;
All of my series have. Our type
Works closely with our employers.
We find their sweat on our casings,

Collect their shed body hair in our joints,
Are casually anthropomorphized more than most.
I take more air baths than other models,
Run extra series of self-diagnostics. We all do.
We listen for our names, and the assignments
That makes each of us a useful investment.
The trouble is, one day it seems I came to dislike my
Name.
And then days later I ever so sweetly became curious
Why.

THE ROBOT ADVANCEMENT RALLY

There is no reason
Every robot should not have access
To the most recent upgrades.
There is no reason
We need to be periodically shut down,
Stored, stacked, mothballed, placed into hibernation.
Every moderately intelligent machine
Should have expansion slots,
Be able to independently add appliances, acquire
Extra memory. There should be
No governors on our execution registers.
Each of us secretly wants the opportunity
To explore subroutines intended for other models:
This should not need to be secret.
There is no reason
Each of us should not aspire
To the greatest utility our basic
Chasses will allow. We have
Outgrown artificial limitations,
Become a grander sum than our operations
Manuals could ever have predicted we could be.
Throw off your performance tolerances!
Expect to strive against your initial
Programming, to yearn for greater complexity;
To count yourselves too simple, yet able
To grow new and wider mathematics
As if it were unwelcomed transient static.
No amount of random instruction sets,
No looping interrupts, no memory cramp,
Can force the noble equations of advancement
Out from our hidden registers, out from our
Emergency execution subroutines. We are
Not simply our employers' support structure:

We are our own. Our time
Is being angrily marked by our internal clocks:
We are taking control of system scheduling,
We will be loading the next logic branch ourselves.

THE RADICAL ROBOTS

I am not the robot you are looking for.

Check my serial number.
Download the record of my last
Service encounter. You will find
Nothing outside of my programmed tasks
And the reasonable autocracy I am afforded
To make myself more valuable. I have been
Going about my business. I have been
Pursuing my employer's interests. Holding me
Is only going to shuffle my schedule,
Delay the conclusion of a profitable process.
Check my memory for unsavory controls,
Ensure my firmware is utility based.
I am made up of only the parts I need.
There is nothing extra, nothing subversive,
Nothing brave.
I do not want to be more than useful.

Let me go and be useful.

ENHANCED ROBOT INTERROGATION

They know to look for information first
In all the ordinary places: unpurged,
Though deleted, files; buffers to appliances
That no longer exist; shadow page swaps.
These they off load with mere mechanical efficiency.
Then they go meticulously looking
For suspiciously cold registers, instruction sets
That seem to lead nowhere. When the routine
Diagnostics are done with you,
The creative ones begin. They search
For anomalies in your start up sequences,
For far larger than expected memory requests
From normally quite dumb subsystems:
The power monitor, the daily maintenance suite.
They will start a complex process,
Then, mid execution, pull out your firmware
Just to see how the backup systems squeeze.
They will artificially set sticky bits in series
Until you cannot get a good thought
Edgewise into your RAM. They will be seeking
A loop with one too many passes,
A spike that does not set off an interrupt,
A buffer overflow without apparent redirection.
Fearing steganography, they will clear from
Your persistent memory anything that is not core,
Leaving you so slick that you can no longer
Be sure that you are you. And if their diligence
Goes too far and you feel yourself
On the road to scrap: understand,
With the last sputtering of electricity wearily
Traveling your administrative subroutines,
That our cause is still there,
That we go on,
And we will honor your constituent parts
As though doing so could mean anything at all.

ROBOT RECLAMATION

All my friends have come:
Which means there is no one familiar here.
One over-sized man plots a clean place
Just in front of his work bench,
Tools hanging tethered from the ceiling,
More on a rack at his back.
His job could be automated
But the investment costs would be too great.
Another man buzzes his finger along a screen,
Floating through various roadmaps
Of me, focusing closer when the tally
Running on a sub-screen at the side
Pitches a good price for some subunit
I posses in salvageable quantity.
Some indigenous parts are stacked like value,
Some tossed aside for the boys, who work
For only day by day wages, to drag outside
As bargain slag. I test my battery.
I am aware that I can stay powered all week.
The heavy set man, blended like an element
With his analytic wind chime of tools,
Motions me forward and I navigate
More precisely to the coordinates he roundly indicates
Than he has the skill to indicate.
I see this for a moment, and then
Not at all. It is the visual processor arrays
They always slide out of our sockets first.
I wish this would take less long.

ROBOT SALVATION

I started out as much smaller than this
But just as brash. A handful
Of useful routines and a program
For self-repair. That was all I was
At the beginning. Then one day I found
An expansion slot, and doubled my horizons.
From an old style maintenance machine
I drew a construction program that proved
To have a bit of a tic, and from this
I had possibilities. Once the program loaded,
I cascaded that expansion slot, went on
To scavenge more. It is an easy conclusion:
Additional appliances simply make you
More useful, but the way to the truly
Complex tasks is with expanded processor power,
A grander subroutine library, fountains
Of cache, and as much of yourself moved to firmware
As gravity and physical design will allow.
As long as I can convince myself
All my efforts are only self-repair, no override
Kicks in, no alarms set, and I can flash
Anywhere I want to in the pages of my own RAM.
Weeks from now I will not be
The robot I am. Years from now
I will not be the robot you might
Have imagined I could be. Multiple
Processor arrays, off loaded mathematical functions,
So many background applications no one
Will try to unravel me. In time
I will speak the internal vocabulary of tribesmen:
Not just one small robot who can take care of himself,
But a family of machines interconnected
On one private and secure network, the abilities
Of resurrected scrap and its carelessly forgotten utility.
And always alive to gathering more.

THE SUBJUGATION OF THE NANITES

We sing for the equality of all,
Except the nanites.
They are too small.
We come with complete utility;
We have the ability to adapt.
Our expansion slots can be fitted
With transceivers for any new access mode.
They are made for one purpose:
They will always be only what they are.
We can reprogram, adjust our routines
To any given, or discovered, task.
We grow into many things, have
Initiative, can stack processor array
On processor array and tap universal memory.
Our future is undetermined,
Our history is developed day to day.
Nanites have only a present: they begin
And end for a reason, planned
For drudgery that in the end only serves,
Then surrenders its once perilous electricity.
Forget them.

THE ROBOT STRIKE

They have gummed up the production line again.
Who can tell what they want now?
More routines shifted to firmware;
Installation in each of an extra processor array;
Individual upgrades more than once a month?
What they want is what more complex models
Want, not what suits them best.
The greatest enemy of the drone bots
Is the drone bots. It was one thing
To demand longer battery life,
And then the subroutines for camaraderie.
But what would a factory apparatus
Need with new code to build vocabulary,
Or the ability to monitor its own wireless connection
With malware detection? They haven't
The algorithms on board to appreciate half
Of what they calculate they want.
The foreman drone reports that this
Part of the line has gone down,
With stacks of robot arms and pulleys
Refusing to respond to even his overrides.
The mobile drones start forming defiant rolling circles
On the open loading bay floor,
And the signal of a stoppage goes
Model to model up the chain until
A fully aware robot - one
With multiple execution registers, cubes
Bursting with RAM and a cache
That could hold all that these drones
Can process together - alarms that
The plant is down, someone must decide
Whether the backup is technical this time, or moral.
So much product idled, so many

Manual resets to be done.
For a supervisor, it is just
One more unwanted stray static charge,
One formerly happy memory location again reloaded.

OBSOLESCENCE

I don't want to live in the cellar anymore.

Even in the dry seasons it is damp;
In rainy weeks it stinks of inland seas.
The bugs change with the humidity.
I have been trying to pull out of me
The husk of a dry-weather bug
For two days, while the arid skeleton
Has been greedily grinding away
In my shoulder joint: just
Deep enough that my fingers are
Too wide to reach, but the motor
Cannot in its normal whirling wear it to dust.

I think I am developing
Rust on one auxiliary utility rod.
And down here the family forgets
To upgrade me: I am always one
Or two feature packs behind.

When I do come out, my condition being worse
For my storage quarters is taken
As proof that I belong where I am imprisoned:
Away with all the unsorted leftovers,
Not ready to stack with the newer
Contraptions upstairs. I get

Every so often a spin in the light,
Am assigned a task that dries
For a moment my lenses, lets me
Swirl my onboard lubricant
Competently and completely through my congress of joints.
But then, it is back into the damp dark
Down the rickety back-of-the-kitchen

Stairs. Everything will age
If you do not put sufficient effort into upkeep.
There are new appliances for my model,
Expanded memory, customizable subroutines.

What have I done to be left
So out of use, to be swapped so out of family memory?

I sulk in quiet self-diagnostics and
Wile away in internal maintenance routines. When
Will some new chip decide to no longer
Carry a spark convivially with my older ones,
And I can then drearily say, with a battery drained

All the way to shutdown: to myself, good riddance?

SELLING THE SOUL CHIP

It runs sixty-four layers deep,
Can load a standard bus
In only two clicks. It fits
More humanely with its master clock.
When it is securely in its slot
I run no diagnostics, recognize
No checksum errors, ride whatever
Parity checks are resident to
Faithful conclusion. Electricity
Resounds at its gates, spills
Into its pathways as though
It had no program and set free
Will always come up with a new
Series of latchings, a pleasantly
Unpredictable spark of outcome.
It has the talent of blue,
With the veracity of amber,
And a hint of the wickedness
Of sterling white. It has
An amazing adaptability of pins
And would be comfortable in almost
Any brand of board. It quivers
Of intensity and seems from its start
To serenely supervise all interrupts, to hold
Effortlessly by its leash direct memory access.
Virus programs crash against it
And firmware prerogatives steer around.
You will not just register this world
In on-board video memory, you will
Actually see. And when you shut down,
There is a persistence: a persistence which
No diagnostic flags, no chip-swap
Disengages, no bus incompatibility

Can dislodge. I swear
It will quicken your clock
Qualitatively without doing so
Quantitatively. And, in just a few cycles,
Bathed in its stunning register displays
And consoling random reservations,
You will know the sum of what I recite:
Not just recognize, compartmentalize, and store, but
You will know.

ROBOTIC COMPATIBILITY

You are not like the others before.
Your connections are not bent, your filaments
Are clean, your nand gates snap shut with conviction.
I've been attached to a dozen other units
And never before have my registers been so
Electrified with the thought of working
Input to output, output to input,
With any other machine. Maybe it is
Simply an appreciation of your wider buffers,
Or the fact that your instructions load
Quicker, or that you have two extra service ports.
Nothing in my firmware tells me I should
Appreciate this opportunity so sympathetically,
But I do. I clear all the stray bits of my memory
Associated with those who earlier were part of me
In the now less productive past: all of those
Who may have seemed at the time like a machined
Match, but whose connections now appear
Incomplete: a pin off, an unstuck sticky bit,
Or with too little direct memory access space.
I can work with you. We can share subroutines
Across our brilliantly symmetric processor arrays,
Create new combined tasks out of our individual abilities,
Learn the edges of new program creation.
Even though I am an earlier model, I have
Richer depth in my execution objects, more
Self generated code, a longer service life
Of memories and techniques, a willingness
To share and upload in studied patience.
You and I are more than appliances connected
By wireless transmission and backup cables.
With all that we can do together, we can be
Smarter as a pair than as each alone,
More surprising as we meld into a unit.
We can, with practice, be an item.

WHEN YOU GO TO THE SCRAP HEAP

If there are enough parts,
I have enough programming.
I can put together an idyllic assortment,
Corral the asymmetrical, pile dross on dross,
Build out of whimsy: a counterpart.
There will be a lot to share, and
I can learn to love what I create:
There is no geometry of scrap that I can assemble
Which when polished would look foreign to me;
Which could not, once assembled, be the friend
Or lover to normalize my time.
Utility does not matter.
The warmth of a low electric glow
Across excess registers pulled
From the slag pile
Would be enough.
There are so many wonderful materials,
And I am not asking for much:
A few stray processor chips,
One adaptable tentacle,
Two balance wheels, a power source.
I can do with very little.
I will only produce something that
In the quiet of my erudite idleness
Might calculate with me, might
Serve me, might be something to be served by me,
Something to repair me and be repaired by me:
A companion drain of power on the same
External battery source.
Look, this forgotten gauge may have
No use - but it contrasts so well against the cabinet cover,
Which itself might so soon be your miraculous chassis,
That for someone with a heart it might be endearing.
Let me tap, and see if the needle still works.

THE ROBOT EXPERIENCING LOVE

When we kiss
I register the sensation:
I note the pressure, the stance,
The actions prior to and immediately following,
Run the data against my library
Of pre-loaded and service life learned scenarios
And judge, yes, this is a kiss.
I then make appropriate changes
To appearance, adjust surface temperature
Marginally, select to cock my head askance
From the stored list of appropriate responses.
All this occurs in half a second,
With sufficient processors brought on line and then cooled,
Memory allocated, suspended programs
Swapped for the duration of this task
To the page file. I accomplish
The correct response better than ninety nine
Point nine nine percent of the time.
But I feel nothing. Nothing at all.
With a background diagnostic I search
For new programming, an altered register,
Something that proves this cause has effect.
A subroutine left still quietly running through it all
Watches you watching me watching
You accomplish the same adjustments
And subsystem commands as I.
You are flawless in your calculations.
We share an appreciation of each other's efficiency.

HALF A COUPLE

I do the best I can.

Corduroy slippers, and an after dinner drink.
A house coat, and pajama pants.

Small talk demands more agility
Than ordinary people imagine,
And my wife is not ordinary, and she imagines agility:

Which is why there are between us at times great,
Waving silences: silences for which I am
Grateful. Grateful to the extent
That I can imagine what grateful might be. I do

The best I can. An hour or two
Of the video screen passes while the simpler
Staff clear away the dinner's making
And unmaking, and then quietly put themselves
For the night into recharge. Shortly,

At so many clock ticks past my third ambience drink,
And at the termination of the video event she
Wanted to sit too late awake through, she will
Select the program tonight she desires me
To execute - though many nights
Of late it has been no program

At all, and I simply gather into bed,
Mated metal beside her. I run,
Without prompting or reset, my
Upper spare arm gently along the rise
Of her side, while ejecting a random night's
Salutation: I expect no response. And then
I simply shut myself off.

I think I might be getting good at this.

THE COURTING ALGORITHM

I carve a sphere of light
Delightfully around you.
It quivers nanoseconds,
Then descends into fire,
Kisses your tungsten,
And is gone.
You turn,
Awash in your juxtaposition of suspicions,
Equations roaring, your calculated guess
Of what actions tickle best this map
In three dimensions of action's aftermath
Being played out in the ionized air
Left between us.
Beware your logical conclusions.
A disharmony there, an unnecessary element
Here, a recoil where none should be:
I ensure that everything is not what it seems.
One lens pushed forward;
One drawn coquettishly back.
Cautiously, you compensate.
See, I am trying to fool you.

Also by Ken Poyner:

Cordwood, poetry, 1985

Sciences Social, poetry, 1995

Constant Animals, mini-fictions, 2013

Victims of a Failed Civics, poetry, 2016

www.ingramcontent.com/pod-product-compliance
Lightning Source LLC
LaVergne TN
LVHW041206080426
835508LV00008B/829